The Sayings of Lao Tzu

The Sayings of Lao Tzu
by Lao Tzu
Translated by Lionel Giles

A & D Publishing
PO Box 3005
Radford VA 24143-3005
www.wilderpublications.com

ISBN 10: 1-60459-302-4
ISBN 13: 978-1-60459-302-0
First Edition

Table of Contents

EDITORIAL NOTE

THE object of the Editors of this series is a very definite one. They desire above all things that, in their humble way, these books shall be the ambassadors of good-will and understanding between East and West—the old world of Thought and the new of Action. In this endeavour, and in their own sphere, they are but followers of the highest example in the land. They are confident that a deeper knowledge of the great ideals and lofty philosophy of Oriental thought may help to a revival of that true spirit of Charity which neither despises nor fears the nation of another creed and colour.

L. CRANMER-BYNG.
S. A. KAPADIA.
NORTHBROOK SOCIETY,
21, CROMWELL ROAD,
KENSINGTON, S.W.

INTRODUCTION

WITH rare modesty and intelligent self-appreciation, Confucius described himself as "a transmitter, not a maker, one who loved and believed in the ancients." This judicious estimate fairly sums up the position of China's most prominent teacher. Incalculable though his influence has been over millions of the human race, it is due rather to his sterling common sense backed by the moral strength of his character, than to any striking intellectual power or novelty in his ideas.

But some fifty years before the time of Confucius there lived another great Chinaman, who, besides being a lover of antiquity, takes high rank as a profound and original thinker. Apart from the thick crop of legend and myth which soon gathered round his name, very little is known about the life and personality of Lao Tzu, and even the meagre account preserved for us in the history of Ssu-ma Ch'ien must be looked upon with suspicion. All the alleged meetings and conversations with Confucius may safely be rejected, not only on account of chronological difficulties, but because they are exactly the sort of invention which would to likely to pass current in an early and uncritical age. We need not, however, go so far as those who impugn the very existence of Lao Tzu as an individual, and regard the book which passes under his name as a mere collection of scraps of ancient proverbial philosophy. Some colour, indeed, is lent to this theory by the uncertainty that attaches to the proper interpretation of the name Lao Tzu, which is variously explained as (1) Old Boy, because he is said to have been born with a white beard (but we may rather suspect that the story was invented to explain the name); (2) Son of Lao, this being the surname of the virgin mother who conceived him at the sight of a falling star; or (3) Old Philosopher, because of the great age at which he wrote his immortal book, the Tao Tê Ching.

The mention of this classic, or "Treatise of the Way and of Virtue" (as it may be translated for want of better English equivalents), brings us naturally to the vexed question as to whether the text which has come down to us can really be attributed to the hand of Lao Tzu, or whether it is not rather a garbled and unauthorised compilation of his sayings, or even the mere forgery of a later age. The Chinese themselves, it may be remarked, are almost unanimous in denying its authenticity. It has been urged that we must make allowance here for Confucian bias; but the internal evidence alone should suffice to dispel the notion, to which many eminent sinologues have clung, that the Tao Tê Ching in its present form can possibly represent the actual work of Lao Tzu. On the other hand, it is highly probable that much of it is substantially what he said or wrote, though carelessly collected and pieced together at random. Ssu-ma Ch'ien, who published his history in 91 B.C., and was consequently removed from Lao Tzu by a much longer period than we are from Shakespeare, tells us that the Sage wrote a book of five thousand and odd words; and, indeed, by that time the Tao Tê Ching may possibly have existed in something like its present shape. But anyone who reflects on the turbulent condition of China during the intervening centuries, and the chaotic state of primitive literature before the labours of Confucius, to say nothing of the Burning of the Books in 213 B.C., will find it hard to convince himself that Ssu-ma Ch'ien ever had before him the actual writings of the philosopher.

Arbitrary and confused though the arrangement of the Tao Tê Ching appears, it is possible to trace a coherent line of thought throughout the whole. And although no coiner of paradox on such an extensive scale as Lao Tzu could hope to achieve absolute and invariable consistency, it is easy to see that the Tao Tê Ching is something more than a mere jumble of stray aphorisms—that it is, in fact, the well-defined though rudimentary outline of a great system of transcendental and ethical philosophy. That this magnificent scheme of thought never reached its full expression in Lao Tzu's treatment is largely due to the fact that he was perpetually struggling to convey his ideas through the medium of a language still imperfectly developed, and forming an inadequate vehicle for abstruse philosophical conceptions. This, too, combined with an extraordinary conciseness of diction, is the cause of the obscurity which hangs over several portions of the text, and which the labours of innumerable commentators have done very little to clear away. To the wide scope thus afforded for the imagination we owe the startling discoveries, in the body of the work, of the Doctrine of the Trinity, and of the Hebrew word for Jehovah, thinly disguised in its Chinese dress. Sad to say, both of these once famous theories are now totally discredited.

The real value of the Tao Tê Ching lies not in such puerilities, but in its wealth of suggestive hints and pregnant phrases, each containing a world of thought in itself and capable of expansion into volumes. Whether Lao Tzu ever developed the germs of thought thrown out with such prodigality, we do not know. At any rate, no record of the development remains. And if Lao Tzu failed to work out his own system, the task was never satisfactorily accomplished by those who came after him. It is true that an enormous superstructure of Taoist literature has been raised upon the slender foundation of the Tao Tê Ching, but these Taoist writers soon forsook the austerity of Lao Tzu's way for the more attractive fields of ritual and magic. Lao Tzu was a Socrates who never found a Plato or an Aristotle to reap the goodly harvest he had sown; even Chuang Tzu, the greatest of his followers, whose exquisite literary style contrasts strangely with the rugged sentences of the Tao Tê Ching, scarcely seems to have caught the true spirit of his Master, and is apt to lose himself in the vague speculations of a dreamy mysticism.

Lao Tzu's work, however, was able to command attention on its own merits. It was first officially recognised as a "canon" or "classic" under the Emperor Ching Ti (B.C. 156-140) of the Han Dynasty, after which the study of Tao survived many vicissitudes, being now under a cloud, and now again in high favour at Court. One Emperor was in the habit of holding forth on the doctrines of Lao Tzu before his assembled ministers, and would forthwith degrade any one who stretched, yawned, or spat during his discourse. Another published an edition of the Tao Tê Ching, which is described in the preface as "the root of all things, the teacher of kings, and the most precious jewel of the public." The first Emperor of the later Chin dynasty asked if Tao was of any use in government. Chang Ch'ien-ming told him that "with Tao a corpse could govern the Empire." By successive edicts the Tao Tê Ching was made obligatory at the examination for graduates of the second degree, every one was required to possess a copy of the work, and it was cut on stone at both capitals. Later on, printed copies were distributed to all directors of education, and it was translated into the language of the Nü-chên Tartars. Finally, Kublai Khan ordered all Taoist books to be burnt, with the exception of the Tao Tê Ching, thus showing a just appreciation of the gulf separating Lao Tzu from the later writers on Tao.

In view of the disjointed and inartistic character of the work, and its antagonism to many of the principles of orthodox Confucianism, it is small wonder that native scholars, with true Chinese subordination of matter to form, seldom profess to hold it in great esteem; and, indeed, its qualities are not such as would strongly appeal to an essentially hard-headed and materialistic race. Yet, on reflection, it will certainly appear that the teaching of Lao Tel has not been barren of practical results. The great political lesson of laisser-faire is one that the Chinese people has well assimilated and perhaps carried to excess; it may even be said to impregnate their national life more thoroughly than any doctrine of Confucius. From two great evils of modern civilisation—the bane of over-legislation and the pest of meddlesome and overbearing officialdom—China is remarkably free; and in few other countries does the individual enjoy such absolute liberty of action. Thus, on the whole, the Chinese may be said to have adopted Lao Tzu's main principles of government, with no small success. It is hard to believe that a rigidly despotic Empire, encumbered with an irksome array of laws and statutes, could have remained homogeneous and intact throughout so lengthy a period. Who can doubt that the enormous bulk of China has managed to defy the disintegrating action of time by reason of its very inertness and placidity? It has been suggested that Lao Tzu may have reached this doctrine of non-interference by observing that the Supreme Power, Tao, governs the Universe by fixed laws, and yet leaves to man an apparently unrestricted freedom of will. Be this as it may, he was undoubtedly the first man to preach the gospel of peace and intelligent inaction, being in this, as in many other respects, far in advance of his age.

In those troublous times, when the land was torn by internecine feuds, and the spirit of militarism was rife, it is not a little remarkable to find him expressing unqualified abhorrence of war, though, to be sure, this was but the logical outcome of his system of quietism. Few can help being struck by the similarity of tone between the sayings of Lao Tzu and the Gospel enunciated six centuries later by the Prince of Peace. There are two famous utterances in particular which secure to Lao Tzu the glory of having anticipated the lofty morality of the Sermon on the Mount. The cavillers who would rank the Golden Rule of Confucius below that of Christ will find it hard to get over the fact that Lao Tzu said, "Requite injury with kindness," and "To the not-good I would be good in order to make them good." It was a hundred and fifty years later that Plato reached the same conclusion in the first book of the Republic.

It is interesting to observe certain points of contact between Lao Tzu and the early Greek philosophers. He may be compared both with Parmenides, who disparaged sense-knowledge and taught the existence of the One as opposed to the Many, and with Heraclitus, whose theory of the identity of contraries recalls some of our Sage's paradoxes. But it is when we come to Plato that the most striking parallels occur. It has not escaped notice that something like the Platonic doctrine of ideas is discoverable in the "forms" which Lao Tzu conceives as residing in Tao. But, so far as I know, no one has yet pointed out what a close likeness Tao itself bears to that curious abstraction which Plato calls the Idea of the Good. The function and attributes of this grandiose conception are not set forth quite so fully or clearly as those of Tao, but it certainly covers a great deal more than the ordinary moral connotation of our word "good." [1] It is at once the creative and sustaining Cause of the Universe, the condition of all knowledge, and the Summum Bonum or supreme object of man's desire. Being a metaphysical entity, it cannot be perceived by the eye or ear of sense, and is therefore ridiculed by the inferior man of little intelligence, while only the few can enter into close communion with it. Now, all of this might stand equally well as a description of Tao. On the other hand, the inactivity and repose which are so insisted on by the Chinese thinker as the primary characteristics of Tao, would have been less intelligible to the Greek, and seem to bring us nearer to Buddhism.

The lack of reliable information about Lao Tzu is very disappointing. One cannot help wishing that some of the less important details touching the life of Confucius could be exchanged for an authentic personal account, however brief, of his older contemporary. All that we know for certain is that, after having spent most of his life in the State of Chou, he set out at an advanced age towards the West, passed the frontier, and was never heard of again. Thus Lao Tzu's gigantic figure looms but indistinctly through the mist of ages, and to gather some idea of his personality we must be content to fall back on his own rough-hewn sentences. There is one striking passage in which he describes himself, half sarcastically and half in earnest, as a dullard and a clown compared with ordinary men, and this, he seems to indicate, is the result of his adherence to Tao. These words, evidently written in great bitterness of spirit, may have been wrung from him by a sense of his failure to convert the careless generation which would have none of the Tao he venerated as the most precious thing under heaven. In showing himself, the man of Tao, in such a disadvantageous light, his meaning was probably much the same as that of Plato in the allegory of the Cave, where he depicts the blindness and bewilderment of those who descend once more into the darkness of their prison after having contemplated the dazzling brilliance of the sun.

Lao Tzu's despondency would have been greater still, could he have foreseen how his pure and idealistic teaching was destined to be dragged in the mire of degrading superstition, which for centuries has made Taoism a byword of reproach. Though frequently described as one of the "three religions of China," this cult is really little more than an inextricable mass of jugglery and fraud, absorbed from various popular beliefs and other sources, including even the rival creed of Buddhism, and conducted by a body of priests recruited from the very dregs of the Empire. Such a fate, however, is less to be wondered at than deplored, seeing that the great Founder himself took no pains to establish a practicable system. He propounded lofty sentiments, and neglected the homely details without which his ideas could not bear fruit. Moreover, when all is said and done, idealism can never hope to hold its own in human affairs, until indeed the new era dawns of which Plato dreamed long ago, and this world of ours becomes ripe for the dominion of Philosopher-Kings.

1, WILLCOTT ROAD, ACTON,
June 21, 1904.

Footnotes

[1] Lao Tzu, like Plato, recognizes very little distinction between Knowledge and Virtue, the rational and moral sides of man's nature. Virtue with him is simply the knowledge of Tao, just as with Plato it is the knowledge of "the Good."

TAO IN ITS TRANSCENDENTAL ASPECT, AND IN ITS PHYSICAL MANIFESTATION

THE Tao which can be expressed in words is not the eternal Tao; the name which can be uttered is not its eternal name. Without a name, it is the Beginning of Heaven and Earth; with a name, it is the Mother of all things. Only one who is eternally free from earthly passions can apprehend its spiritual essence; he who is ever clogged by passions can see no more than its outer form. These two things, the spiritual and the material, though we call them by different names, in their origin are one and the same. This sameness is a mystery,—the mystery of mysteries. It is the gate of all spirituality.

How unfathomable is Tao! It seems to be the ancestral progenitor of all things. How pure and clear is Tao! It would seem to be everlasting. I know not of whom it is the offspring. It appears to have been anterior to any Sovereign Power. [1]

Tao eludes the sense of sight, and is therefore called colourless. It eludes the sense of hearing, and is therefore called soundless. It eludes the sense of touch, and is therefore called incorporeal. These three qualities cannot be apprehended, and hence they may be blended into unity.

Its upper part is not bright, and its lower part is not obscure. Ceaseless in action, it cannot be named, but returns again to nothingness. We may call it the form of the formless, the image of the imageless, the fleeting and the indeterminable. Would you go before it, you cannot see its face; would you go behind it, you cannot see its back.

The mightiest manifestations of active force flow solely from Tao.

Tao in itself is vague, impalpable,—how impalpable, how vague! Yet within it there is Form. How vague, how impalpable! Yet within it there is Substance. How profound, how obscure! Yet within it there is a Vital Principle. This principle is the Quintessence of Reality, and out of it comes Truth.

From of old until now, its name has never passed away. It watches over the beginning of all things. How do I know this about the beginning of things?

Through Tao.

There is something, chaotic yet complete, which existed before Heaven and Earth. Oh, how still it is, and formless, standing alone without changing, reaching everywhere without suffering harm! It must be regarded as the Mother of the Universe. Its name I know not. To designate it, I call it Tao. Endeavouring to describe it, I call it Great.Being great, it passes on; passing on, it becomes remote; having become remote, it returns.

Therefore Tao is great; Heaven is great; Earth is great; and the Sovereign also is great. In the Universe there are four powers, of which the Sovereign is one. Man takes his law from the Earth; the Earth takes its law from Heaven; Heaven takes its law from Tao; but the law of Tao is its own spontaneity.

Tao in its unchanging aspect has no name. Small though it be in its primordial simplicity, mankind dare not claim its service. Could princes and kings hold and keep it, all creation would spontaneously pay homage. Heaven and Earth would unite in sending down sweet dew, and the people would be righteous unbidden and of their own accord.

As soon as Tao creates order, it becomes nameable. When it once has a name, men will know how to rest in it. Knowing how to rest in it, they will run no risk of harm.

Tao as it exists in the world is like the great rivers and seas which receive the streams from the valleys.

All-pervading is the Great Tao. It can be at once on the right hand and on the left. All things depend on it for life, and it rejects them not. Its task accomplished, it takes no credit. It loves and nourishes all things, but does not act as master. It is ever free from desire. We may call it small. All things return to it, yet it does not act as master. We may call it great.

The whole world will flock to him who holds the mighty form of Tao. They will come and receive no hurt, but find rest, peace, and tranquillity.

With music and dainties we may detain the passing guest. But if we open our mouths to speak of Tao, he finds it tasteless and insipid.

Not visible to the sight, not audible to the ear, in its use it is inexhaustible.

Retrogression is the movement of Tao. Weakness is the character of Tao.

All things under Heaven derive their being from Tao in the form of Existence; Tao in the form of Existence sprang from Tao in the form of Non-Existence.

Tao is a great square with no angles, a great vessel which takes long to complete, a great sound which cannot be heard, a great image with no form.

Tao lies hid and cannot be named, yet it has the power of transmuting and perfecting all things.

Tao produced Unity; Unity produced Duality; Duality produced Trinity; and Trinity produced all existing objects. These myriad objects leave darkness behind them and embrace the light, being harmonised by the breath of Vacancy.

Tao produces all things; its Virtue nourishes them; its Nature gives them form; its Force perfects them.

Hence there is not a single thing but pays homage to Tao and extols its Virtue. This homage paid to Tao, this extolling of its Virtue, is due to no command, but is always spontaneous.

Thus it is that Tao, engendering all things, nourishes them, develops them, and fosters them; perfects them, ripens them, tends them, and protects them.

Production without possession, action without self-assertion, development without domination this is its mysterious operation.

The World has a First Cause, which may be regarded as the Mother of the World. When one has the Mother, one can know the Child. He who knows the Child and still keeps the Mother, though his body perish, shall run no risk of harm.

It is the Way of Heaven not to strive, and yet it knows how to overcome; not to speak, and yet it knows how to obtain a response; it calls not, and things come of themselves; it is slow to move, but excellent in its designs.

Heaven's net is vast; though its meshes are wide, it lets nothing slip through.

The Way of Heaven is like the drawing of a bow: it brings down what is high and raises what is low. It is the Way of Heaven to take from those who have too much, and give to those who have too little. But the way of man is not so. He takes away from those who have too little, to add to his own superabundance. What man is there that can take of his own superabundance and give it to mankind? Only he who possesses Tao.

The Tao of Heaven has no favourites. It gives to all good men without distinction.

Things wax strong and then decay. This is the contrary of Tao. What is contrary to Tao soon perishes.

Footnotes

[1] This sentence is admittedly obscure, and it may be an interpolation. Lao Tzu's system of cosmogony has no place for any Divine Being independent of Tao. On the other hand, to translate ti by "Emperor," as some have done, necessarily involves us in an absurd anti-climax.

TAO AS A MORAL PRINCIPLE, OR "VIRTUE"

THE highest goodness is like water, for water is excellent in benefiting all things, and it does not strive. It occupies the lowest place, which men abhor. And therefore it is near akin to Tao.

When your work is done and fame has been achieved, then retire into the background; for this is the Way of Heaven.

Those who follow the Way desire not excess; and thus without excess they are for ever exempt from change.

All things alike do their work, and then we see them subside. When they have reached their bloom, each returns to its origin. Returning to their origin means rest or fulfilment of destiny. This reversion is an eternal law. To know that law is to be enlightened. Not to know it, is misery and calamity. He who knows the eternal law is liberal-minded. Being liberal-minded, he is just. Being just, he is kingly. Being kingly, he is akin to Heaven. Being akin to Heaven, he possesses Tao. Possessed of Tao, he endures for ever. Though his body perish, yet he suffers no harm.

He who acts in accordance with Tao, becomes one with Tao. He who treads the path of Virtue becomes one with Virtue. He who pursues a course of Vice becomes one with Vice. The man who is one with Tao, Tao is also glad to receive. The man who is one with Virtue, Virtue is also glad to receive. The man who is one with Vice, Vice is also glad to receive.

He who is self-approving does not shine. He who boasts has no merit. He who exalts himself does not rise high. Judged according to Tao, he is like remnants of food or a tumour on the body—an object of universal disgust. Therefore one who has Tao will not consort with such.

Perfect Virtue acquires nothing; therefore it obtains everything. Perfect Virtue does nothing, yet there is nothing which it does not effect. Perfect Charity operates without the need of anything to evoke it. Perfect Duty to one's neighbour operates, but always needs to be evoked. Perfect Ceremony operates, and calls for no outward response; nevertheless it induces respect. [1]

Ceremonies are the outward expression of inward feelings.

If Tao perishes, then Virtue will perish; if Virtue perishes, then Charity will perish; if Charity perishes, then Duty to one's neighbour will perish; if Duty to one's neighbour perishes, then Ceremonies will perish.

Ceremonies are but the veneer of loyalty and good faith, while oft-times the source of disorder. Knowledge of externals is but a showy ornament of Tao, while oft-times the beginning of imbecility.

Therefore the truly great man takes his stand upon what is solid, and not upon what is superficial; upon what is real, and not upon what is ornamental. He rejects the latter in favour of the former.

When the superior scholar hears of Tao, he diligently practises it. When the average scholar hears of Tao, he sometimes retains it, sometimes loses it. When the inferior scholar hears of Tao, he loudly laughs at it. Were it not thus ridiculed, it would not be worthy of the name of Tao.

He who is enlightened by Tao seems wrapped in darkness. He who is advanced in Tao seems to be going back. He who walks smoothly in Tao seems to be on a rugged path.

The man of highest virtue appears lowly. He who is truly pure behaves as though he were sullied. He who has virtue in abundance behaves as though it were not enough. He who is firm in virtue seems like a skulking pretender. He who is simple and true appears unstable as water.

If Tao prevails on earth, horses will be used for purposes of agriculture. If Tao does not prevail, war-horses will be bred on the common.

If we had sufficient knowledge to walk in the Great Way, what we should most fear would be boastful display.

The Great Way is very smooth, but the people love the by-paths.

Where the palaces are very splendid, there the fields will be very waste, and the granaries very empty.

The wearing of gay embroidered robes, the carrying of sharp swords, fastidiousness in food and drink, superabundance of property and wealth:—this I call flaunting robbery; most assuredly it is not Tao.

He who trusts to his abundance of natural virtue is like an infant newly born, whom venomous reptiles will not sting, wild beasts will not seize, birds of prey will not strike. The infant's bones are weak, its sinews are soft, yet its grasp is firm. All day long it will cry without its voice becoming hoarse. This is because the harmony of its bodily system is perfect.

Temper your sharpness, disentangle your ideas, moderate your brilliancy, live in harmony with your age. This is being in conformity with the principle of Tao. Such a man is impervious alike to favour and disgrace, to benefits and injuries, to honour and contempt. And therefore he is esteemed above all mankind.

In governing men and in serving Heaven, there is nothing like moderation. For only by moderation can there be an early return to man's normal state. This early return is the same as a great storage of Virtue. With a great storage of Virtue there is naught which may not be achieved. If there is naught which may not be achieved, then no one will know to what extent this power reaches. And if no one knows to what extent a man's power reaches, that man is fit to be the ruler of a State. Having the secret of rule, his rule shall endure. Setting the tap-root deep, and making the spreading roots firm: this is the way to ensure long life to the tree.

Tao is the sanctuary where all things find refuge, the good man's priceless treasure, the guardian and saviour of him who is not good.

Hence at the enthronement of an Emperor and the appointment of his three ducal ministers, though there be some who bear presents of costly jade and drive chariots with teams of four horses, that is not so good as sitting still and offering the gift of this Tao.

Why was it that the men of old esteemed this Tao so highly? Is it not because it may be daily sought and found, and can remit the sins of the guilty? Hence it is the most precious thing under Heaven.

All the world says that my Tao is great, but unlike other teaching. It is just because it is great that it appears unlike other teaching. If it had this likeness, long ago would its smallness have been known.

The skilful philosophers of the olden time were subtle, spiritual, profound, and penetrating. They were so deep as to be incomprehensible. Because they are hard to comprehend, I will endeavour to describe them.

Shrinking were they, like one fording a stream in winter. Cautious were they, like one who fears an attack from any quarter. Circumspect were they, like a stranger guest; self-effacing, like ice about to melt; simple, like unpolished wood; vacant, like a valley; opaque, like muddy water.

When terms are made after a great quarrel, a certain ill-feeling is bound to be left behind. How can this be made good? Therefore, having entered into an agreement, the Sage adheres to his obligations, [2] but does not exact fulfilment from others. The man who has Virtue attends to the spirit of the compact; the man without Virtue attends only to his claims.

He who tries to govern a kingdom by his sagacity is of that kingdom the despoiler; but he who does not govern by sagacity is the kingdom's blessing. He who understands these two sayings may be regarded as a pattern and a model. To keep this principle constantly before one's eyes is called Profound Virtue. Profound Virtue is unfathomable, far-reaching, paradoxical at first, but afterwards exhibiting thorough conformity with Nature.

Footnotes

[1] Han Fei Tzu explains the passage by pointing out that "Virtue is the achievement of Tao; Charity is the glory of Virtue; Duty is the translation into action of Charity; and Ceremony is the ornamental part of Duty."

[2] Literally, "he holds the left-hand portion of the agreement." In olden times, the terms of a contract were inscribed on a wooden tablet, the debit or obligations being on the left, and the credit or dues on the right; it was then broken in two, and each of the contracting parties kept his own half until

fulfilment was demanded, when the validity of the claim was tested by fitting the two halves together.

THE DOCTRINE OF INACTION

THE Sage occupies himself with inaction, and conveys instruction without words. Is it not by neglecting self-interest that one will be able to achieve it?

Purge yourself of your profound intelligence, and you can still be free from blemish. Cherish the people and order the kingdom, and you can still do without meddlesome action.

Who is there that can make muddy water clear? But if allowed to remain still, it will gradually become clear of itself. Who is there that can secure a state of absolute repose? But let time go on, and the state of repose will gradually arise.

Be sparing of speech, and things will come right of themselves.

A violent wind does not outlast the morning; a squall of rain does not outlast the day. Such is the course of Nature. And if Nature herself cannot sustain her efforts long, how much less can man!

Attain complete vacuity, and sedulously preserve a state of repose.

Tao is eternally inactive, and yet it leaves nothing undone. If kings and princes could but hold fast to this principle, all things would work out their own reformation. If, having reformed, they still desired to act, I would have them restrained by the simplicity of the Nameless Tao. The simplicity of the Nameless Tao brings about an absence of desire. The absence of desire gives tranquillity. And thus the Empire will rectify itself.

The softest things in the world override the hardest. That which has no substance enters where there is no crevice. Hence I know the advantage of inaction.

Conveying lessons without words, reaping profit without action,—there are few in the world who can attain to this!

Activity conquers cold, but stillness conquers heat. Purity and stillness are the correct principles for mankind.

Without going out of doors one may know the whole world; without looking out of the window, one may see the Way of Heaven. The further one travels, the less one may know. Thus it is that without moving you shall know; without looking you shall see; without doing you shall achieve.

The pursuit of book-learning brings about daily increase. The practice of Tao brings about daily loss. Repeat this loss again and again, and you arrive at inaction. Practise inaction, and there is nothing which cannot be done.

The Empire has ever been won by letting things take their course. He who must always be doing is unfit to obtain the Empire.

Keep the mouth shut, close the gateways of sense, and as long as you live you will have no trouble. Open your lips and push your affairs, and you will not be safe to the end of your days.

Practise inaction, occupy yourself with doing nothing.

Desire not to desire, and you will not value things difficult to obtain. Learn not to learn, and

you will revert to a condition which mankind in general has lost.

Leave all things to take their natural course, and do not interfere.

LOWLINESS AND HUMILITY

ALL things in Nature work silently. They come into being and possess nothing. They fulfil their functions and make no claim.

When merit has been achieved, do not take it to yourself; for if you do not take it to yourself, it shall never be taken from you.

Follow diligently the Way in your own heart, but make no display of it to the world.

Keep behind, and you shall be put in front; keep out, and you shall be kept in.

Goodness strives not, and therefore it is not rebuked.

He that humbles himself shall be preserved entire. He that bends shall be made straight. He that is empty shall be filled. He that is worn out shall be renewed. He who has little shall succeed. He who has much shall go astray.

Therefore the Sage embraces Unity, and is a model for all under Heaven. He is free from self-display, therefore he shines forth; from self-assertion, therefore he is distinguished; from self-glorification, therefore he has merit; from self-exaltation, therefore he rises superior to all. Inasmuch as he does not strive, there is no one in the world who can strive with him.

He who, conscious of being strong, is content to be weak, he shall be the paragon of mankind. Being the paragon of mankind, Virtue will never desert him. He returns to the state of a little child.

He who, conscious of his own light, is content to be obscure,—he shall be the whole world's model. Being the whole world's model, his Virtue will never fail. He reverts to the Absolute.

He who, conscious of desert, is content to suffer disgrace,—he shall be the cynosure of mankind. Being the cynosure of mankind, his Virtue then is full. He returns to perfect simplicity.

He who is great must make humility his base. He who is high must make lowliness his foundation. Thus, princes and kings in speaking of themselves use the terms "lonely," "friendless," "of small account." Is not this making humility their base?

Thus it is that "Some things are increased by being diminished, others are diminished by being increased." What others have taught, I also teach; verily, I will make it the root of my teaching.

What makes a kingdom great is its being like a down-flowing river,—-the central point towards which all the smaller streams under Heaven converge; or like the female throughout the world, who by quiescence always overcomes the male. And quiescence is a form of humility.

Therefore, if a great kingdom humbles itself before a small kingdom, it shall make that small kingdom its prize. And if a small kingdom humbles itself before a great kingdom, it shall win over that great kingdom. Thus the one humbles itself in order to attain, the other attains because it is humble. If the great kingdom has no further desire than to bring men together and to nourish them, the small kingdom will have no further desire than to enter the service of the other. But in order that both may have their desire, the great one must learn humility.

The reason why rivers and seas are able to be lords over a hundred mountain streams, is that they know how to keep below them. That is why they are able to reign over all the mountain streams.

Therefore the Sage, wishing to be above the people, must by his words put himself below them; wishing to be before the people, he must put himself behind them. In this way, though he has his place above them, the people do not feel his weight; though he has his place before them, they do not feel it as an injury. Therefore all mankind delight to exalt him, and weary of him not.

The Sage expects no recognition for what he does; he achieves merit but does not take it to himself; he does not wish to display his worth.

I have three precious things, which I hold fast and prize. The first is gentleness; the second is frugality; the third is humility, which keeps me from putting myself before others. Be gentle, and you can be bold; be frugal, and you can be liberal; avoid putting yourself before others, and you can become a leader among men.

But in the present day men cast off gentleness, and are all for being bold; they spurn frugality, and retain only extravagance; they discard humility, and aim only at being first. Therefore they shall surely perish.

Gentleness brings victory to him who attacks, and safety to him who defends. Those whom Heaven would save, it fences round with gentleness.

The best soldiers are not warlike; the best fighters do not lose their temper. The greatest conquerors are those who overcome their enemies without strife. The greatest directors of men are those who yield place to others. This is called the Virtue of not striving, the capacity for directing mankind; this is being the compeer of Heaven. It was the highest goal of the ancients.

GOVERNMENT

NOT exalting worth keeps the people from rivalry. Not prizing what is hard to procure keeps the people from theft. Not to show them what they may covet is the way to keep their minds from disorder.

Therefore the Sage, when he governs, empties their minds and fills their bellies, weakens their inclinations and strengthens their bones. His constant object is to keep the people without knowledge and without desire, or to prevent those who have knowledge from daring to act. He practises inaction, and nothing remains ungoverned.

He who respects the State as his own person is fit to govern it. He who loves the State as his own body is fit to be entrusted with it.

In the highest antiquity, the people did not know that they had rulers. In the next age they loved and praised them. In the next, they feared them. In the next, they despised them.

How cautious is the Sage, how sparing of his words! When his task is accomplished and affairs are prosperous, the people all say: "We have come to be as we are, naturally and of ourselves."

If any one desires to take the Empire in hand and govern it, I see that he will not succeed. The Empire is a divine utensil which may not be roughly handled. He who meddles, mars. He who holds it by force, loses it.

Fishes must not be taken from the water: the methods of government must not be exhibited to the people.

Use uprightness in ruling a State; employ stratagems in waging war; practise non-interference in order to win the Empire. Now this is how I know what I lay down:—

As restrictions and prohibitions are multiplied in the Empire, the people grow poorer and poorer. When the people are subjected to overmuch government, the land is thrown into confusion. When the people are skilled in many cunning arts, strange are the objects of luxury that appear.

The greater the number of laws and enactments, the more thieves and robbers there will be. Therefore the Sage says: "So long as I do nothing, the people will work out their own reformation. So long as I love calm, the people will right themselves. If only I keep from meddling, the people will grow rich. If only I am free from desire, the people will come naturally back to simplicity."

If the government is sluggish and tolerant, the people will be honest and free from guile. If the government is prying and meddling, there will be constant infraction of the law. Is the government corrupt? Then uprightness becomes rare, and goodness becomes strange. Verily, mankind have been under delusion for many a day!

Govern a great nation as you would cook a small fish. [1]

If the Empire is governed according to Tao, disembodied spirits will not manifest supernatural powers. It is not that they lack supernatural power, but they will not use it to hurt mankind. Again, it is not that they are unable to hurt mankind, but they see that the Sage also does not hurt mankind. If then neither Sage nor spirits work harm, their virtue converges to one beneficent end.

In ancient times those who knew how to practise Tao did not use it to enlighten the people, but rather to keep them ignorant. The difficulty of governing the people arises from their having too much knowledge.

If the people do not fear the majesty of government, a reign of terror will ensue.

Do not confine them within too narrow bounds; do not make their lives too weary. For if you do not weary them of life, then they will not grow weary of you.

If the people do not fear death, what good is there in using death as a deterrent? But if the people are brought up in fear of death, and we can take and execute any man who has committed a monstrous crime, who will dare to follow his example?

Now, there is always one who presides over the infliction of death. He who would take the place of the magistrate and himself inflict death, is like one who should try to do the work of a master-carpenter. And of those who try the work of a master-carpenter there are few who do not cut their own hands.

The people starve because those in authority over them devour too many taxes; that is why they starve. The people are difficult to govern because those placed over them are meddlesome; that is why they are difficult to govern. The people despise death because of their excessive labour in seeking the means of life; that is why they despise death.

A Sage has said: "He who can take upon himself the nation's shame is fit to be lord of the land. He who can take upon himself the nation's calamities is fit to be ruler over the Empire."

Were I ruler of a little State with a small population, and only ten or a hundred men available as soldiers, I would not use them. I would have the people look on death as a grievous thing, and they should not travel to distant countries. Though they might possess boats and carriages, they should have no occasion to ride in them. Though they might own weapons and armour, they should have no need to use them. I would make the people return to the use of knotted cords. [2] They should find their plain food sweet, their rough garments fine. They should be content with their homes, and happy in their simple ways. If a neighbouring State was within sight of mine—nay, if we were close enough to hear the crowing of each other's cocks and the barking of each other's dogs—the two peoples should grow old and die without there ever having been any mutual intercourse.

Footnotes

[1] Q.d., Don't overdo it.

[2] The old quipo method of recording events, before the invention of writing.

WAR

HE who serves a ruler of men in harmony with Tao will not subdue the Empire by force of arms. Such a course is wont to bring retribution in its train.

Where troops have been quartered, brambles and thorns spring up. In the track of great armies there must follow lean years.

The good man wins a victory and then stops; he will not go on to acts of violence. Winning, he boasteth not; he will not triumph; he shows no arrogance. He wins because he cannot choose; after his victory he will not be overbearing.

Weapons, however beautiful, are instruments of ill omen, hateful to all creatures. Therefore he who has Tao will have nothing to do with them.

Where the princely man abides, the weak left hand is in honour. But he who uses weapons honours the stronger right. Weapons are instruments of ill omen; they are not the instruments of the princely man, who uses them only when he needs must. Peace and tranquillity are what he prizes. When he conquers, he is not elate. To be elate were to rejoice in the slaughter of human beings. And he who rejoices in the slaughter of human beings is not fit to work his will in the Empire.

On happy occasions, the left is favoured; on sad occasions, the right. The second in command has his place on the left, the general in chief on the right. That is to say, they are placed in the order observed at funeral rites. And, indeed, he who has exterminated a great multitude of men should bewail them with tears and lamentation. It is well that those who are victorious in battle should be placed in the order of funeral rites.

A certain military commander used to say: "I dare not act the host; I prefer to play the guest. [1] I dare not advance an inch; I prefer to retreat a foot."

There is no greater calamity than lightly engaging in war. Lightly to engage in war is to risk the loss of our treasure. [2]

When opposing warriors join in battle, he who has pity conquers.

Footnotes

[1] According to Chinese etiquette, it is for the master of the house to make advances, and his guest follows suit. Thus "host" here means the one who takes the initiative and begins the attack; "guest," the one who acts on the defensive. The passage may be merely figurative, illustrating the conduct of those who practise Tao.

[2] I.e., humanity or gentleness, mentioned above as one or "three precious things."

PARADOXES

AMONG mankind, the recognition of beauty as such implies the idea of ugliness, and the recognition of good implies the idea of evil. There is the same mutual relation between existence and non-existence in the matter of creation; between difficulty and ease in the matter of accomplishing; between long and short in the matter of form; between high and low in the matter of elevation; between treble and bass in the matter of musical pitch; between before and after in the matter of priority.

Nature is not benevolent; with ruthless indifference she makes all things serve their purposes, like the straw dogs we use at sacrifices. The Sage is not benevolent: he utilises the people with the like inexorability.

The space between Heaven and Earth,—is it not like a bellows? It is empty, yet inexhaustible; when it is put in motion, more and more comes out.

Heaven and Earth are long-lasting. The reason why Heaven and Earth can last long is that they live not for themselves, and thus they are able to endure.

Thirty spokes unite in one nave; the utility of the cart depends on the hollow centre in which the axle turns. Clay is moulded into a vessel; the utility of the vessel depends on its hollow interior. Doors and windows are cut out in order to make a house; the utility of the house depends on the empty spaces.

Thus, while the existence of things may be good, it is the non-existent in them which makes them serviceable.

When the Great Tao falls into disuse, benevolence and righteousness come into vogue. When shrewdness and sagacity appear, great hypocrisy prevails. It is when the bonds of kinship are out of joint that filial piety and paternal affection begin. It is when the State is in a ferment of revolution that loyal patriots arise.

Cast off your holiness, rid yourself of sagacity, and the people will benefit an hundredfold. Discard benevolence and abolish righteousness, and the people will return to filial piety and paternal love. Renounce your scheming and abandon gain, and thieves and robbers will disappear. These three precepts mean that outward show is insufficient, and therefore they bid us be true to our proper nature;—to show simplicity, to embrace plain dealing, to reduce selfishness, to moderate desire.

A variety of colours makes man's eye blind; a diversity of sounds makes man's ear deaf; a mixture of flavours makes man's palate dull.

He who knows others is clever, but he who knows himself is enlightened. He who overcomes others is strong, but he who overcomes himself is mightier still. He is rich who knows when he has enough. He who acts with energy has strength of purpose. He who moves not from his proper place is long-lasting. He who dies, but perishes not, enjoys true longevity.

If you would contract, you must first expand. If you would weaken, you must first strengthen. If you would overthrow, you must first raise up. If you would take, you must first give. This is called the dawn of intelligence.

He who is most perfect seems to be lacking; yet his resources are never outworn. He who is most full seems vacant; yet his uses are inexhaustible.

Extreme straightness is as bad as crookedness. Extreme cleverness is as bad as folly. Extreme fluency is as bad as stammering.

Those who know do not speak; those who .speak do not know.

Abandon learning, and you will be free from trouble and distress.

Failure is the foundation of success, and the means by which it is achieved. Success is the lurking-place of failure; but who can tell when the turning-point will come?

He who acts, destroys; he who grasps, loses. Therefore the Sage does not act, and so does not destroy; he does not grasp, and so he does not lose.

Only he who does nothing for his life's sake can truly be said to value his life.

Man at his birth is tender and weak; at his death he is rigid and strong. Plants and trees when they come forth are tender and crisp; when dead, they are dry and tough. Thus rigidity and strength are the concomitants of death; softness and weakness are the concomitants of life.

Hence the warrior that is strong does not conquer; the tree that is strong is cut down. Therefore the strong and the big take the lower place; the soft and the weak take the higher place.

There is nothing in the world more soft and weak than water, yet for attacking things that are hard and strong there is nothing that surpasses it, nothing that can take its place.

The soft overcomes the hard; the weak overcomes the strong. There is no one in the world but knows this truth, and no one who can put it into practice.

Those who are wise have no wide range of learning; those who range most widely are not wise.

The Sage does not care to hoard. The more he uses for the benefit of others, the more he possesses himself. The more he gives to his fellow-men, the more he has of his own.

The truest sayings are paradoxical.

MISCELLANEOUS SAYINGS AND PRECEPTS

BY many words wit is exhausted; it is better to preserve a mean. The excellence of a dwelling is its site; the excellence of a mind is its profundity; the excellence of giving is charitableness; the excellence of speech is truthfulness; the excellence of government is order; the excellence of action is ability; the excellence of movement is timeliness.

He who grasps more than he can hold, would be better without any. If a house is crammed with treasures of gold and jade, it will be impossible to guard them all.

He who prides himself upon wealth and honour hastens his own downfall. He who strikes with a sharp point will not himself be safe for long.

He who embraces unity of soul by subordinating animal instincts to reason will be able to escape dissolution. He who strives his utmost after tenderness can become even as a little child.

If a man is clear-headed and intelligent, can he be without knowledge?

The Sage attends to the inner and not to the outer; he puts away the objective and holds to the subjective.

Between yes and yea, how small the difference! Between good and evil, how great the difference!

What the world reverences may not be treated with disrespect.

He who has not faith in others shall find no faith in them.

To see oneself is to be clear of sight. Mighty is he who conquers himself.

He who raises himself on tiptoe cannot stand firm; he who stretches his legs wide apart cannot walk.

Racing and hunting excite man's heart to madness.

The struggle for rare possessions drives a man to actions injurious to himself.

The heavy is the foundation of the light; repose is the ruler of unrest.

The wise prince in his daily course never departs from gravity and repose. Though he possess a gorgeous palace, he will dwell therein with calm indifference. How should the lord of a myriad chariots conduct himself with levity in the Empire? Levity loses men's hearts; unrest loses the throne.

The skillful traveller leaves no tracks; the skillful speaker makes no blunders; the skillful reckoner uses no tallies. He who knows how to shut uses no bolts—yet you cannot open. He who knows how to bind uses no cords—yet you cannot undo.

Among men, reject none; among things, reject nothing. This is called comprehensive intelligence.

The good man is the bad man's teacher; the bad man is the material upon which the good man works. If the one does not value his teacher, if the other does not love his material, then despite their sagacity they must go far astray. This is a mystery of great import.

As unwrought material is divided up and made into serviceable vessels, so the Sage turns his simplicity [1] to account, and thereby becomes the ruler of rulers.

The course of things is such that what was in front is now behind; what was hot is now cold; what was strong is now weak; what was complete is now in ruin. Therefore the Sage avoids excess, extravagance, and grandeur.

Which is nearer to you, fame or life? Which is more to you, life or wealth? Which is the greater malady, gain or loss?

Excessive ambitions necessarily entail great sacrifice. Much hoarding must be followed by heavy loss. He who knows when he has enough will not be put to shame. He who knows when to stop will not come to harm. Such a man can look forward to long life.

There is no sin greater than ambition; no calamity greater than discontent; no vice more sickening than covetousness. He who is content always has enough.

Do not wish to be rare like jade, or common like stone.

The Sage has no hard and fast ideas, but he shares the ideas of the people and makes them his own. Living in the world, he is apprehensive lest his heart be sullied by contact with the world. The people all fix their eyes and ears upon him. The Sage looks upon all as his children.

I have heard that he who possesses the secret of life, when travelling abroad, will not flee from rhinoceros or tiger; when entering a hostile camp, he will not equip himself with sword or buckler. The rhinoceros finds in him no place to insert its horn; the tiger has nowhere to fasten its claw; the soldier has nowhere to thrust his blade. And why? Because he has no spot where death can enter.

To see small beginnings is clearness of sight. To rest in weakness is strength.

He who knows how to plant, shall not have his plant uprooted; he who knows how to hold a thing, shall not have it taken away. Sons and grandsons will worship at his shrine, which shall endure from generation to generation.

Knowledge in harmony is called constant. Constant knowledge is called wisdom. [2] Increase of life is called felicity. The mind directing the body is called strength.

Be square without being angular. Be honest without being mean. Be upright without being punctilious. Be brilliant without being showy.

Good words shall gain you honour in the market-place, but good deeds shall gain you friends among men.

To the good I would be good; to the not-good I would also be good, in order to make them good.

With the faithful I would keep faith; with the unfaithful I would also keep faith, in order that they may become faithful.

Even if a man is bad, how can it be right to cast him off?

Requite injury with kindness.

The difficult things of this world must once have been easy; the great things of this world must once have been small. Set about difficult things while they are still easy; do great things while they are still small. The Sage never affects to do anything great, and therefore he is able to achieve his great results.

He who always thinks things easy is sure to find them difficult. Therefore the Sage ever anticipates difficulties, and thus it is he never encounters them.

While times are quiet, it is easy to take action; ere coming troubles have cast their shadows, it is easy to lay plans.

That which is brittle is easily broken; that which is minute is easily dissipated. Take precautions before the evil appears; regulate things before disorder has begun.

The tree which needs two arms to span its girth sprang from the tiniest shoot. Yon tower, nine storeys high, rose from a little mound of earth. A journey of a thousand miles began with a single step.

A great principle cannot be divided; therefore it is that many containers cannot contain it. [3]

The Sage knows what is in him, but makes no display; he respects himself, but seeks not honour for himself.

To know, but to be as though not knowing, is the height of wisdom. Not to know, and yet to affect knowledge, is a vice. If we regard this vice as such, we shall escape it. The Sage has not this vice. It is because he regards it as a vice that he escapes it.

Use the light that is in you to revert to your natural clearness of sight. Then the loss of the body is unattended by calamity. This is called doubly enduring.

In the management of affairs, people constantly break down just when they are nearing a successful issue. If they took as much care at the end as at the beginning, they would not fail in their enterprises.

He who lightly promises is sure to keep but little faith.

He whose boldness leads him to venture, will be slain; he who is brave enough not to venture, will live. Of these two, one has the benefit, the other has the hurt. But who is it that knows the real cause of Heaven's hatred? This is why the Sage hesitates and finds it difficult to act.

The violent and stiff-necked die not by a natural death.

True words are not fine; fine words are not true.

The good are not contentious; the contentious are not good.

This is the Way of Heaven, which benefits, and injures not. This is the Way of the Sage, in whose actions there is no element of strife.

Footnotes

[1] There is a play on the word p'u, simplicity, the original meaning of which is "unwronght material."

[2] There must always be a due harmony between mind and body, neither of them being allowed to outstrip the other. Under such circumstances, the mental powers will be constant, invariable, always equally ready for use when called upon. And such a mental condition is what Lao Tzu here calls "wisdom"

[3] That is, a principle which applies to the whole applies also to a part. Because you may divide the containing whole, you are not at liberty to divide the principle.

LAO TZU ON HIMSELF

ALAS! the barrenness of the age has not yet reached its limit. All men are radiant with happiness, as if enjoying a great feast, as if mounted on a tower in spring. I alone am still, and give as yet no sign of joy. I am like an infant which has not yet smiled, forlorn as one who has nowhere to lay his head. Other men have plenty, while I alone seem to have lost all. I am a man foolish in heart, dull and confused. Other men are full of light; I alone seem to be in darkness. Other men are alert; I alone am listless. I am unsettled as the ocean, drifting as though I had no stopping-place. All men have their usefulness; I alone am stupid and clownish. Lonely though I am and unlike other men, yet I revere the Foster-Mother, Tao.

My words are very easy to understand, very easy to put into practice; yet the world can neither understand nor practise them.

My words have a clue, my actions have an underlying principle. It is because men do not know the clue that they understand me not.

Those who know me are but few, and on that account my honour is the greater.

Thus the Sage wears coarse garments, but carries a jewel in his bosom.

CPSIA information can be obtained
at www.ICGtesting.com
Printed in the USA
BVHW07s1721230518
517120BV00006B/676/P

9 781604 593020